SEEING The Getty Center

The decision to build the Getty Center was a defining moment in the transformation of the J. Paul Getty Trust from a small museum with three collections—Greek and Roman antiquities, European paintings, and French decorative arts—to a multifaceted institution comprising the present Museum, five institutes, and a grant program devoted to scholarship, conservation, and education in the visual arts and the humanities. The reasons for that decision were both practical and philosophical.

As the J. Paul Getty Museum expanded its collecting activities to include drawings, illuminated manuscripts, photographs, and sculpture, it became clear that the Getty Villa in Malibu would not provide adequate space to display the collections in ways that would engage visitors. Nor would it allow us to reach out to Southern California's diverse audiences through the imaginative educational programs and facilities that will provide Museum visitors new ways of seeing and enjoying those collections. In addition, as the newly formed Getty Research Institute for the History of Art and the Humanities and Getty Conservation Institute began to define their missions, it became apparent that their ambitious programs would require specialized facilities.

Just as important as those practical considerations were the philosophical ones. It was our conviction from the beginning that each of the Getty organizations could be strengthened by proximity to the others— that by grouping them together in a campuslike setting, we could encourage a spirit of collaboration and an exchange of ideas among scholars, scientists, and educators that would lead to new directions in intellectual inquiry. We concluded that our interdisciplinary efforts could succeed only if we included the Getty Information Institute and the Getty Education Institute for the Arts as well.

Finally, we viewed the creation of the Getty Center as an opportunity to make a significant architectural statement and to create a new and unique cultural resource for the city of Los Angeles. Of all art forms, architecture is the one with which people interact most intimately in the course of their daily lives. It is an art of substance, a language that communicates a society's values through forms and materials. Great architecture possesses a singular power to call people together, shape their interaction, influence their thinking—and foster community. As the twentieth century draws to a close, Los Angeles stands as a crossroads of world cultures. It is only fitting, then, that the Getty Center serve both as a locus of international research in the visual arts and humanities and as a cultural landmark for the people of Los Angeles—a place of intellectual and spiritual renewal, where the experience of art, architecture, and nature speaks to us of both the achievements of the past and the promise of the future.

Harold M. Williams
President and Chief Executive Officer
The J. Paul Getty Trust
December 1997

The Getty Center is, in many senses of the word, about seeing: looking, visiting, discovering, experienci examining, understanding. The Center provides an extraordinary vantage point from which to ga outward over the city of Los Angeles, the Santa Monica and San Gabriel Mountains, and the Paci Ocean, and a position from which to turn inward to contemplate great works of art and the achie ments of the world's diverse cultures. A rare wedding of imagination and pragmatism, the Center pr vides new and diverse perspectives on the act of creativity and the legacy of the artist's endeavor

The vision for the Getty Center grew out of a desire on the part of the J. Paul Getty Trust to make its grow
ing collections and expanding programs accessible to greater numbers of visitors. In 1983, the Tr
purchased more than 700 acres in the southern foothills of the Santa Monica Mountains overlo
ing the Sepulveda Pass, at the nexus of two interstate freeways and several local thoroughfares. W
the selection, in 1984, of Richard Meier as architect for the Getty Center project, plans evolved fo
six-building campus that would bring together the Getty programs and provide both a unique cult
al resource and a vital architectural landmark for the city of Los Angeles. Only a small fraction of t
property has been developed. The Center's main buildings, arrayed along two intersecting ridges,
cupy less than one-quarter of the campus's 24 acres. The remaining grounds have been landscap
to create courtyards, gardens, and terraces or preserved in their natural state.

The Los Angeles to which the Getty Center reaches out is the youngest of America's great cities. Poised the Pacific Rim, and gateway to Mexico and Latin America, Los Angeles has the busiest port comp of any city in the U.S. and is the nation's largest trade center. L.A. is birthplace of the Internet and ho to the entertainment, information, and other new industries that are shaping American culture and as the millennium approaches. An urban laboratory in which many global challenges—environmen issues, economic and social policy concerns, and public education and health care reform—are too being explored, Los Angeles is bound to become a world capital for the twenty-first century. The Ge Center is an unparalleled resource for L.A. as the city achieves cultural maturity and comes into own as the most diverse metropolis on the planet.

A visit to the Getty Center has built-in drama and excitement, beginning with the electric tram trip from the parking garage to the hilltop campus. The brief ride, with its unfolding vistas of the campus above and cityscape below, is its own reward. The journey, moreover, offers vivid evidence of the effort that has been made to preserve much of the site and its natural beauty. Visitors, whether serious students of art or those seeking simple pleasures in the Center's gardens, will find that the ascent to the Arrival Plaza brings them to quite another level.

In a city renowned for its love affair with the automobile and its short supply of public spaces, the Getty Center makes a monumental addition to the civic architecture of Los Angeles. "The architecture," explains Richard Meier, "frames small vignettes and expansive panoramas. It heightens awareness of nature and the city. A place apart, yet firmly connected to the world beyond, the Getty Center is visible, accessible, and open to all."

urteen years in the making, the Getty Center and J. Paul Getty Trust have grown up together. Not only did the Trust's programmatic requirements give direction to the Center's design and construction processes, but the architecture—through its informed response to the site, distinctly modern forms, and refined unity of expression—helped to define the programs and activities it was conceived to house. Located here are the J. Paul Getty Museum, the Getty Research Institute for the History of Art and the Humanities, the Getty Conservation Institute, the Getty Information Institute, the Getty Education Institute for the Arts, the Getty Grant Program, and the Trust's administrative offices. A 450-seat auditorium and a cafe-restaurant with wonderful views make the Center an ideal venue for lectures, films, concerts, gallery talks, and family programs.

Richard Meier has observed that "Architecture is the subject of my architecture" and in the perfectly scal[e]
open expanse of the Getty Center's Arrival Plaza can be seen his unerring sense of order and relian[ce]
on light to shape an environment equally hospitable to nature and art. Meier's affinity for quality a[nd]
permanence, virtues very much in keeping with the Getty Trust's mission, are manifested in his [at]
tention to detail and choice of materials. He selected travertine, a richly nuanced form of limesto[ne,]
to clad the Museum and the bases of other buildings, as well as for paving. The Center's travertin[e—]
some 16,000 tons—was quarried in Bagni di Tivoli, outside of Rome. Blocks used on facades were [cut]
using a special technique to produce a "cleft," or rough, surface; fossilized leaves are visible in plac[es.]
The stone combines human scale and civic grandeur, lending the Center a sense of constancy yet p[ro]
viding a subtly dimensional exterior "curtain" upon which sunlight plays in an ever-changing sh[ow]
of radiance.

The Getty Center affirms the enduring influence on Richard Meier of the Swiss modernist architect Le Corbusier. Flowing, curvilinear elements, echoing the undulations in the natural terrain, are among the distinctive motifs expressed in the Getty Center design. Panels of off-white metal and great expanses of glass give the buildings a fluidity and lightness that belies their mass. But echoes of Frank Lloyd Wright, Richard Neutra, Rudolf Schindler, and Irving Gill—architects who built in the friendly climate of Southern California—are also apparent in the design's embrace of innovations in modern materials and technology and in the ease with which interior and exterior spaces have been integrated. Meier has made the buildings seem almost permeable and the transition from ceiling to sky nearly transparent.

The Getty Center is averse to confinement. The spaces in between structures, whether lush garden or paved passageway, tie together the Center's six buildings and establish a sense of intimacy and human scale. Among the pleasures the architecture provides are innumerable surprises—unexpected views of the city and ocean, intriguing glimpses of one building framing another, layer upon layer of carefully rationalized and finely wrought edifice. The way the Center's buildings relate to each other on their elevated setting recalls the historic hilltowns of Italy, with their alcoves, plazas, and gardens. Though it has strong associations to an age-old tradition of architecture, the Getty Center is very much of its time and place.

In time the gardens at the Getty Center will flourish to reveal their collective variety and individual charm. Among them, the Central Garden is likely to remain a singular attraction and favored retreat. Artist Robert Irwin has created an environment that at once re-establishes the ravine that is a natural feature of the Getty Center site, yet transforms nature into a work of art in its own right. A stream threads its way through the grasses and London plane trees and past the bursts of bougainvillea, spilling over a terraced granite wall before coming to rest in a reflecting pool in which a maze of azaleas seems to float. "My work deals with the experience of things in a constant state of change," Irwin explains. "A garden is changing all the time, with the passing seasons and different times of day—but also moment-to-moment, in response to wind, light, and the presence of people."

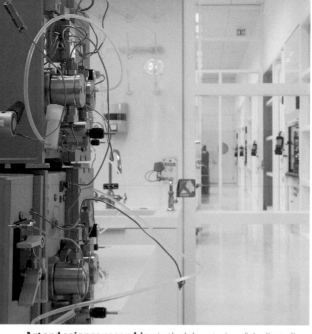

Art and science recombine in the laboratories of the Getty Conservation Institute, where advanced technologies are employed in the service of centuries-old representatives of the world's cultural heritage—whether master paintings, ancient monuments, or historic cities. The work conducted in these labs, in the Center's East Building, helps to preserve irreplaceable landmarks in Africa and Asia, Latin America and the United States, Europe and the Middle East—and to ensure that future generations will still be able to enjoy the artistic achievements of the past.

Getty Center's cohesive sense of place, the quality of the space inside and outside its buildings, and of the light that enlivens the entire complex, are certain to become the signal virtues for which the Center is known. Such acuity is a hallmark of Richard Meier's work; he has received the Pritzker Prize, architecture's greatest honor, as well as the gold medals of the American Institute of Architects and the Royal Institute of British Architects, and the 1997 Praemium Imperiale Award, from the Japan Art Association, for outstanding lifetime achievement in the arts.

The architecture of the Getty Center presents an ongoing dialogue between natural and built forms. Extensive landscaping of the site—8,000 trees have been planted here, enough to populate a modest-size forest—seamlessly ties untouched outlying chaparral to formal plantings surrounding the Center and the carefully structured gardens inside the campus proper. Native, drought-tolerant materials (cactus, succulents), and transplants from other locales (Italian stone pines, tropical palms) work sometimes in harmony with, and sometimes in counterpoint to, the architecture; cool colors on the shady northern slopes grow warmer as the site opens to the sun and then deepen into a desert palette at the southernmost promontory.

Located on the southwest part of the campus, the building housing the Research Institute is, but for a cutaway quarter, a circular structure. There are a small public exhibition space and reading room near the entrance of this building, but as the locale for scholarly research, it is conceived as a more private, focused space. "Its circular shape, transparent and open to the city, reflects both the introspection of individual research and its connection with broader audiences," observes Salvatore Settis, the Institute's director. Shelves of reference materials and reading areas spiral around a central courtyard; scholars can work in private offices or at open stations intermixed with the resources in various parts of the building. "The design," explains Settis, "invites an active exchange of ideas among scholars and students and encourages them to explore new forms of research."

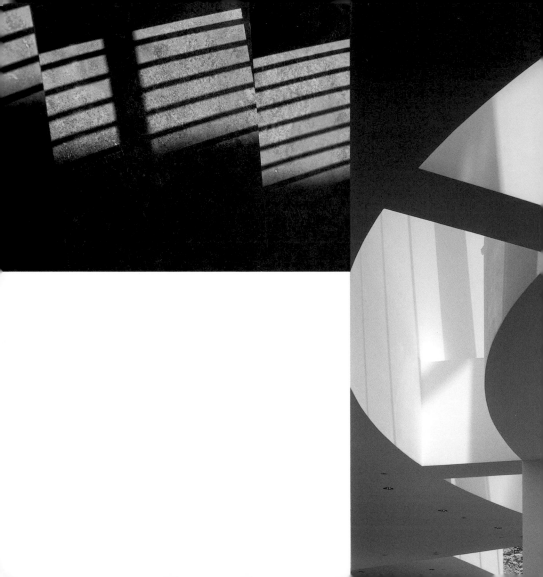

The J. Paul Getty Museum profits from twenty-first-century construction techniq
and exhibition technology yet preserves the intimacy and warmth afforded
the great nineteenth-century galleries. As envisioned by John Walsh, the
seum's director, and designed by Richard Meier, the new Museum compri
a series of two-story pavilions clustered around an open courtyard. The
floor of each of the five pavilions contains skylighted paintings galleries; o
orative arts, illuminated manuscripts, photographs, and other light-sensi
works are displayed on the lower level. "Our first requirement was for
leries that would flatter the collections with excellent light, good proporti
and no distractions," says Walsh. Of equal importance was a plan that wo
allow visitors a variety of options in routing their own tour of the collecti
and provide them pleasant indoor and outdoor places for rest and refreshm

The Museum, the largest and most public of all the Getty Center buildings, fuses modernist rigor with classical values of balance, clarity, and moderation. The broad stairway leading to the entrance, the stone walls, the terraces, pergola and enclosed walkways—these are contemporary adaptations of the traditional. The cylindrical rotunda of the Entrance Hall provides inviting views onto the courtyard, the gallery pavilions, and the Central Garden, which lies between the Museum and the Research Institute. The interplay and flow from interior to exterior spaces makes this a congenial and relaxed museum, in tune with the sensibilities of Southern California life, while the restraint and dignity of the exhibition spaces ensure that the architecture enhances, rather than competes with, the works of art.

"Natural daylight, lively and abundant, is what artists paint-ed by and figured into their calculations for the experi-ence of the audience," observes John Walsh. And so the Getty Museum has been built to recreate the most de-sirable conditions for looking at paintings. The Muse-um's 20 paintings galleries have skylights and coved ceilings to distribute light; a computerized system of louvers, timed to the movement of the sun across the sky, allows the galleries to receive optimal illumination for the protection of the paintings and enjoyment of viewers. "Daylight brings out subtleties of color and tex-ture that the artists themselves could see in their stu-dios," says Walsh. "Electric light is no substitute."

the summit of a city constantly redefining itself, the Getty Center takes its place with the Hollywood sign and the Griffith Park Observatory as an enduring hilltop emblem. "The completion of the Getty Center is not the end of a process, but a beginning," observes Harold M. Williams. "In the decades ahead, the Getty must remain alert and responsive to all the communities it serves." The integrated architecture of the campus promises a renewed spirit of collaboration and intellectual inquiry among the scholars, scientists, and educators who animate the Getty's programs. Visitors will be drawn again and again to an uncommon environment in which art, architecture, and nature combine to exhilarate the human spirit. An energizing and enriching cultural resource for all of Los Angeles, the Getty Center delivers a heightened experience of seeing.